Limited Engagement

poems by

Joanne Greenway

Finishing Line Press
Georgetown, Kentucky

Limited Engagement

*for Theresa Eugenia,
who gave me light
and
Clarence David,
who always let me shine*

Copyright © 2016 by Joanne Greenway
ISBN 978-1-944899-40-0 First Edition
All rights reserved under International and Pan-American Copyright Conventions. No part of this book may be reproduced in any manner whatsoever without written permission from the publisher, except in the case of brief quotations embodied in critical articles and reviews.

ACKNOWLEDGMENTS

"Smoking" was previously published online on the website of the Hamilton County / City of Cincinnati Public Library.

My appreciation, first and foremost, to the members of the Greater Cincinnati Writers League for midwifing these poems to fruition, especially my dear friend Jerry Judge. Their generosity of spirit was invaluable to me.

I would also like to thank my aunt, Anna Pontecorvo, my Italian language expert and family historian.

My sincere thanks to David Shough and Karen Gaski, my photographers, and Hershel Dunne, for his computer expertise.

Editor: Christen Kincaid

Cover Art: David Shough

Author Photo: Karen Gaski

Cover Design: Elizabeth Maines

Printed in the USA on acid-free paper.
Order online: www.finishinglinepress.com
also available on amazon.com

Author inquiries and mail orders:
Finishing Line Press
P. O. Box 1626
Georgetown, Kentucky 40324
U. S. A.

Table of Contents

Dog Dreams 1
Valve Job 2
In the Subway 3
Ten Years Gone 4
Ladies First 5
Atonement 6
The Hunter 7
Nonna Mia 8
Nonna at the Speedway 10
Smoking 12
Limited Engagement 13
I Saw It Coming 14
The Fourth of July 16
Automat Memories 17
Hair Wars 19
Beauty and the Breast 21
Lines 23
The Barbie Mystique 25
Dancing for Miss Patti 27
Pas de Chat 29
Mystery in Aisle 23 30
Sunday Rundown 31
Good Candy 32
Confessions of a Part-time Mourner 33
Breakfast at Half Day Café 35
Polar Vortex 37

DOG DREAMS

He thuds to the floor
and parks himself
across the doorsill.
This fur-bearing wall
will keep me safe
from all intruders.

Sleep comes quickly to him.
His sonorous snore recalls
a 40-watt generator, and
his belly heaves
like a bellows
fanning his reverie.

Soon comes a burst
of whimpers and whines,
the thrashing of legs
as he pursues rabbits
across his dreamscape.
Or is it he who is hunted
in his unknowable world?

When I open my eyes,
I still feel fright from
vexing dreams of being
trapped, lost or cast
into unbounded darkness.
He is at my bedside,
snorting and chuffing.
His entire body
vibrates with joy—
no memory of
his own dreams.

A chill hangs in the air
as I make my way
out of the room.
My bare feet warm
in his heat shadow.

VALVE JOB

A pig has unwillingly donated
the spare part necessary
to keep my ticker ticking.
I have given up a leg vein
for two bypasses.
But wait, there's more.
By week's end a pacemaker
will be implanted in my chest.

Waking up in the ICU
after a death-like slumber,
I attempt to speak,
but the anesthesia
has nearly struck me dumb.
What comes out is fluent gibberish.

I survey my ravaged body.
My wounds are glued shut,
and I am wound
with yards of bandages.
My neck and belly have sprouted
so many tubes and wires,
I conjure an image of Medusa.

Sleep is no more possible here
than in a casino game room.
Bells, buzzers, alarms, pagers
and chatter from the nurses' station
keep me from my rest.
Throughout the night,
a procession of shadows
will probe, poke and puncture.
I pray for the intercession of morphine.

IN THE SUBWAY

She was maybe in her thirties.
Hair tied back, no make-up.
Fairly kempt, I thought,
for a down-and-outer.
Sliding doors whooshed shut
and before the train
got fully under way,
she launched "the pitch."
In a voice easily heard
over the subway's roar,
she gave us the backstory:
illness, debt, job loss.
The IND was their home now.
Please, folks… anything you can spare…
She produced a Starbuck's cup
and passed it around the car.
Most people kept their money,
but my friend obliged,
parting with two dollars.
Sucker! I thought.
She is unwise to the ways
of City hucksters.
But she insisted, clearly impressed:
That woman could go into sales—
so prepared, so market-savvy.
That takes guts, you know?
After circulating unmolested
the cup found its way back to her.
Quickly, she surfed the waves
of rush hour commuters,
disappearing into the next car.
I could not help but wonder
what kind of nut she made
from her daily E train shake-down
—and if I'd ever have the nerve
to ask for what I want.

TEN YEARS GONE

Unlike life, Spring Grove
goes on forever.
Stately obelisks,
ornate tombs and
Temples of Diana
dress the dirt homes
of our illustrious dead.
The beauty of this place
holds the living in thrall,
making them loath to leave.

I used to get lost
searching for your spot.
Now I know you sleep
among the Gypsies,
whose large headstones
and flashy floral sprays
are impossible to miss.

I wish I could have given
you a Gypsy send-off:
a flower bedecked carriage
drawn by white horses,
a shower of gold coins
as they laid you in the earth
in a grey gabardine suit,
to make you presentable
in the sweet hereafter.

But, like Thelonious,
you played improv and
favored unique headgear—
bill caps and tams,
trilbies and pork pies.
I buried the maroon
Béret Basque with your ashes.

I leave a few smooth stones
on your rose granite slab.

LADIES FIRST

She was making breakfast
on the old gas range.
Its oven door had fallen off
years ago. When she fell,
the impact of her body on
the faded linoleum was
enough to wake the old man.
Later, I heard him say he thought
she had dropped something.
In her final moments, I wonder
if she fretted that he would miss
his short stack and sausages
more than he would her.

This was not the natural
order of things. Who would
take care of him now?
Clean his house? Cook his
meals on the old stove
he had refused to replace?
She finally stopped begging
for a new one—or anything
else she wanted, just so
he couldn't tell her no.
Over fifty-seven years,
she got used to being
denied and dismissed,
always coming in last.

This time…
she got to go first.

ATONEMENT

When it was still a sport
and my father still a hunter,
he filled his quarry bag with pheasant.
Long ago, they flew free—
never planted or pen-raised.

How it pained me, the sight
of these birds lying
lifeless on old newspapers,
their jewel-like feathers fanned
across our kitchen table. Still…

I watched like a little ghoul
as my city-bred mother
plucked and gutted them.
In their stomachs I found
a Last Supper of seeds and pebbles.

She singed their pinfeathers
over a gas burner, bathed
them in a red wine marinade.
I tasted only remorse;
I had seen their suffering.

To honor their martyrdom,
I built a crude shrine to them
in my little blue bedroom:
two elegant tail feathers
in a Mason jar reliquary.

The fields and marshes where
wild pheasant once ruled
have yielded to subdivisions
and strip malls. Only
the drab wild turkey flourishes.
They cook up tough.
No one covets their plumage.

THE HUNTER

In his cracked, weathered hands
brother held the shiny gold cylinder.
It looked like a tube of lipstick,
but it was a bullet he'd crafted
for his single-shot deer rifle.
He could launch this gem
from five hundred yards and
Bambi would never know what hit him.
This ammo, fired quietly from his
single-shot Thompson Encore,
would produce only a whistle.
His quarry would not startle
or have time to bolt.

In this still wild place
deer hunting is a religion,
Buck heads adorn the walls
of almost every home.
Truant officers expect boys
to ditch school to go hunting.
It is a common sight to see deer
hanging from trees by their hind legs,
ready to be butchered before
ending up on the dinner table
as venison chops in Port wine sauce.

There are too many deer, brother says,
and hunting saves them from starving.
His features soften when he describes
a recent encounter with a deer family,
a doe and two freckled fawns.
The female stuck close to her mother
but the male gamboled about,
full of curiosity and mischief.
The sight of them so charmed him,
brother decided to let their Mama live.

This time.

NONNA MIA

Nothing that passed
for real conversation
ever came between us.
After 60 years in America,
her accent was still so thick
you could cut it with a *biscotto*.

She looked and moved
as if she'd been born old.
I can still see her shuffling
around the East Harlem apartment:
shapeless cotton housedress,
long, grey hair knotted at her neck.

My most pungent memories
require no subtitles:
pinches that stung my cheeks,
frilly doll clothes sewn by hand,
heaps of honeyed *struffoli*,
sprinkled with nonpareils.

But my Nonna had other "gifts," too.
She was the neighborhood Oracle
who could pour molten wax
into a pan of cold water,
then read the shapes, the way
other seers read tea leaves.
I heard scary stories of poltergeists
and exorcisms from the Old Country.
She showed me how to ward off
the *malocchio* by signing
devil's horns with my fingers.

Every night after dinner,
she'd settle down in her rocker
to pray her fifteen decade rosary
and watch wrestling matches on TV.
Her idol was a prancing, barefoot Argentine,
a stalwart son of Italy, Antonino Rocca.

At intervals, she'd interrupt her prayers
to urge Nino: "Give it 'a him!"
If his adversary got the upper hand,
she'd curse him with, *Fidendo*!

Rocca would rebound
with headstand scissor holds,
spectacular flying kicks and
his trade-marked back-breaker!

I marveled at her capacity
to embrace the sacred
and the profane with equal fervor,
often in the same breath.

Perhaps she saw Rocca as
some sort of saint in Speedos,
a near bare-assed Great Equalizer.
It was Good versus Evil
every Saturday night.
Nino hardly ever failed to throttle
an endless string of bullies.
It never would have occurred
to her to question his record
for, in Nonna's mind, Nino was
like the Pope—infallible.

NONNA AT THE SPEEDWAY

I remember race nights, back
in the Fifties, when Dad
would drive us to Rhinebeck
Speedway where cousin
Butch raced the Sweet 16,
a '36 Chevy Coupe with a
six-cylinder Chrysler Spitfire
engine. Her silver shell was
tagged with gallows humor:
Undertaker's Special was
my favorite, and the most apt.

On one of our outings we
brought along our Nonna,
up from the City for a visit.
I wondered how this woman,
a rosary praying, maker of
ravioli from scratch, would take
to the frenzy of stock car racing.
She had come to America from
the lemon-scented Amalfi Coast
as a teen-aged bride. Now,
she sat with us in the front bleachers
huffing air laced with grime,
grease and gasoline.

It was understood we were there
to root for the Sweet 16.
Butch's girlfriend, steady Evy,
led the family cheering squad.
But Nonna didn't understand
about rooting for the home team.
Suddenly, above the roar,
we heard, *Avanti, trenta-tre!*
Thirty-three was a flamed
maroon and gold crate
that surged past the Sweet 16
and clung to the lead—
though only for a few laps.

We never asked Nonna
why she favored the flashy 33.
Besides, her crude English
would not have been up to it.

Her life had been one long,
dull grind in low gear: nine
children, endless work, no play.
Until tonight! In my fantasy,
Nonna, seduced by engine roar
and burning rubber, bolts from
her seat and climbs the fence
to ride shotgun in number 33.
It turns out the driver is the
identical twin of her idol,
wrestler Antonino Rocca.

He gives her the ride of her life.

SMOKING

I cannot help but smile
at the memory of my mother
standing at the bathroom mirror,
ripe with red lipstick,
as she smoked a cigarette.
The head tilt, the sidelong glance—
she was flirting with her reflection,
as she practiced looking sultry.
Silver screen beauty
framed in graceful plumes.

My cigarettes came in candy form
in a faux Lucky Strike box:
sweet, slender little sticks,
red-tipped at one end.
I wanted to smolder like my mother,
wear open-toed high heels
that made a tock-tock on the sidewalk.
I sneaked real cigarettes in our orchard,
channeling Rita Hayworth, until
my throat closed and my eyes watered.

On the Classic Movies channel
Hayworth still heats up the screen,
exhaling curls of smoke as thick
and sexy as her auburn mane.
Her elegant handling of a cigarette
unmatched to this day.

I gave up smoking long ago,
settling for wholesome over glamorous,
wear only sensible shoes,
noiseless on the pavement.

LIMITED ENGAGEMENT

In our storied careers, we embraced every role:
restrained and sober, slapstick and screwball.
The critics hailed the performers as fearless,
losing ourselves in every role,
nailing every scene in a single take.
Siskel and Ebert would have given us
two thumbs up… way up.

We rarely strayed from the script,
but we could ad lib when we had to.
And, once in a while, we could not resist
the sheer melodrama of a good fight scene.
No stunt or body doubles for us—
we took our lumps just like the pros.

We never knew where we were in the arc
of our story—at times, we had to improvise.
Then one day, Death swept the boards,
chewed the scenery to bits and pieces
and rang the curtain down.

Up and down Broadway
marquee lights went dark.

I SAW IT COMING

The husband greets me
with a silent nod.

Once inside the reading room,
I find Miriam in a trance.
Her eyelids flutter and twitch.
Such tics cannot be faked;
she is the real deal.
When she comes to,
my seer invites me to sit.
We join hands in silent prayer
so The Light may come
to her consciousness.
In a few minutes,
she will spill forth
everything I want to know;
everything I want to hear.

But she disappoints.
The man in my life has "issues,"
she warns; I need to move on.
Fixing me with her open gaze,
she counsels forbearance:
a new man will soon enter my life,
perhaps in the fall.
Though I seem to recall,
at my last reading, she told me
it would be this spring.
But psychics, she had explained,
can never give dates certain.

My future is a wrap in twenty minutes.
She rises serenely from her chair,
ushers me from the room.
I cross through the front parlor,
where the flannel-shirted husband
sits glued to his spot on the sofa,
caressing his briarwood pipe.
A nimbus of bitter smoke
hovers over him.
I decide he reminds me
of a whipped dog,
restive, plotting his escape.

He grouses briefly
about our testy spring weather.
I drive home, forty dollars lighter,
looking forward to the fall.

Weeks later, I run into my Sybil
when our carts intersect
in the produce aisle of the IGA.
Instantly, she blurts her awful news:
He's gone.
He had another woman.
It's been going on for years.

THE FOURTH OF JULY

Back porch-sitting in the dark,
the wet, warm air of summer
is my cloak. I await the next breeze
as eagerly as a lover's touch.

The soft boom of fireworks
rises from the riverfront,
the air soon pungent
with the scent of gun powder.

From my lawn chair, I take in
another kind of spectacle
unfolding against the curtain of night:
fireflies strobe all around me.

Only the males light up,
flashing for no other reason
than to attract a mate—
a clever system, I think.

Long ago, on summer nights
I pursued them through high grass
just to hold their light captive
in my cupped hands,
if only for a while.

I lean back and listen
to the rise and fall of cricket song
while hundreds of tiny love-lights
flicker in the blackness,
each one a plea for connection.

AUTOMAT MEMORIES

My mother and I must have
made the trip from Grandma's
house in Queens into Manhattan
at least a hundred times.
I loved the noisy, bouncy
train ride as much as the
Rockettes, the Empire State
or the playground called Macy's.
When it came time for lunch,
only the Automat would do.

It stood on the corner
of Third and Forty-third,
a vast rectangle filled
with square, lacquered tables,
marble, marquetry and mayhem.
"Nickel throwers" wearing
little rubber cots on their fingers
changed your dollars into coins.
Along a 35-foot wall
you fed them into slots
next to little glass chambers,
then turned the chrome-plated knob.
A little door opened and there stood
your chicken salad sandwich
or slice of coconut cream pie.

The Automat was so famous,
it even had a cameo role
in an old Doris Day movie.
Audrey Meadows played
a vengeful Automat worker
who reached through the wall
to land a stinging slap
to the face of Rock Hudson.

But nothing was ever
automatic at the Automat.
It was fated to die young,
brought down by high overhead
and the fast food juggernaut.

In a recurring dream,
I have written a sequel
to *That Touch of Mink*.

Rock Hudson and I
canoodle over coffee,
the Automat's own special
drip-brewed blend.
Forget good girl Doris,
I tell him—s*he's not your type.*
I empty my change purse,
slide all my nickels across the table
and tell him nothing heals a broken
heart like coconut cream pie.

HAIR WARS

My mother used to wash
my hair in Breck Shampoo.
To keep the soap out of my eyes
she had me lie down
on her ironing board,
head hanging over the sink.

After my ordeal,
she stood me on the sink
to let me draw pictures
in the steamy mirror.
Through my towel turban
I heard muffled endearments:
Such a pretty little girl!

Until, one day, proof
of my imperfections
came by way of Tonette.
My poker-straight Buster Brown
was banished in favor of curls
that bounced as I walked
but snarled in Mother's comb.
Bring on the creme rinse!
My hair was a shame without Tame.
Oh, I remember the mane
when my determined mother
battled my mutinous locks.

My Neapolitan nonna
never cut her long, dark hair.
Wore it washer-woman style,
anchored with a few combs.
When she took them out,
it unfurled to her knees.
I tried to grow mine that long,
but abandoned the quest
when the headaches started.
My hair had become…
unmanageable.

I sought relief from Mr. Freddie
who wore a cheap toupée
and a rapacious smile.
He removed my barrettes,
then flinched when my escaping hair

exploded like a smoke bomb.
He sighed audibly at the challenge
and even made the sign of the Cross.

Ever since, my crowning glory
barely grazes my collar,
no longer the stuff to inspire men
to run barefoot through it.
A practical and compliant coif,
it is layered and lacquered
into a brown helmet,
every hair subdued,
some gone to grey.

These days, I almost like
what I see in the mirror
until *she* intrudes:
gleaming, glacial,
single strand of pearls.
Inscrutable smile.

In my wrathful fantasy
I snatch her bald-headed,
but the Breck Girl vanishes
in a cloud of cornsilk:
a blonde *Joconde*
who never served a hitch
in the Hair Wars.

BEAUTY AND THE BREAST

I

A man will check out
a woman's rack before
making eye contact.
Six hundred grams
of fat are all it takes
to feed a fantasy.
Women always find fault:
too big, too small, lacking
in perkiness or symmetry.
They do not understand
anything over a handful
or a mouthful is wasted.

II

I still chafe at the memory
of my first training bra.
This attempt to train my breasts
was an unqualified failure;
my breasts still refuse
to stand at attention.

III

In some cultures, it takes
a bosom to be a buddy.
Eastern European Gypsies
ascribe no sexuality to breasts.
They are nothing more
than a set of milk cans.
Gypsy women greet each other
with a friendly tit tweak.

IV

A mastectomy patient
told her plastic surgeon
to preserve her nipples
for reconstruction.
To keep the tissue alive
he grafted them
to her inner thighs.

Picasso would have
parked them on her face
and painted her portrait.

V

Then there was the
shocked young mother
who discovered
her nursing toddler
let go of her breast
to take stealthy bites
of his 'Nilla wafer.
Milk and cookies are
still his favorite snack.

VI

Some men never recover
from early weaning.
In bed at night
adolescent boys
hunker under sheets
with flashlights
and forbidden magazines,
making ever more
memories of mammaries.

Years later, as new fathers,
they profess jealousy
of their suckling babes.
They cannot bear
the flagrant reminder:
they are no longer safe.

LINES

The lunch rush is over,
so I sit in this café
to read as long as I like
and indulge my guilty pleasure
of eavesdropping
on the unsuspecting.

At the next table, two women
rail against the scourge of aging.
As I pore over my book,
they pour forth their woes
about the state of their pores.
The enemy has struck
on many fronts:
crows' feet,
collagen loss,
orange peel skin,
and marionette lines.
They discuss their arsenal:
designer scarf camo,
the blessings of Botox,
fat injections
and chemical peels.
I am tempted to turn
and check them out.
I then decide to ask
if they've seen our waiter.

*Honey, I have no idea
where that man is,*
the older one replies.
An arch of waxed brows
is all the expression
her frozen face can summon.
I imagine her receiving tragic news
of a lover lost to a cruel death.
But where would grief take refuge
with no folds or creases to settle in?
And what of laughter that leaves no lines?
There lingers no trace of
dues paid in joys and sorrows.

Her vacant visage
reminds me of an

old store front:
façade still intact,
it invites nothing but curiosity.

THE BARBIE MYSTIQUE

For her eighth birthday, my
closest friend received
the best present ever:
a Barbie Doll. A doll that
could not walk or talk,
whose sole purpose was
to look chic and sexy.

Undressed, she was
female perfection: perky
neoprene bosoms, long,
coltish legs, blonde hair
and blazing baby blues.
Feet made for stilettos and
a body for spandex and sparkle.
She led many charmed lives:
princess, nightclub chantoozy,
stewardess, cheerleader,
and had a special outfit for each
sex role stereotype.

My shapeless little body bore
no resemblance to hers.
I wore big girls' clothes.
Chubbette was my label,
my nickname, and my shame.

Over the next fifty years,
I dyed, curled, and straightened,
wore crippling high heels,
dieted and brutalized
my joints in Jazzercise,
raised my flaccid breasts
to new heights with
industrial-strength bras
and spent a princely sum
on make-up and wardrobe—
in quest of the Barbie Ideal.

Fifty years post-Barbie,
I have lost collagen and bounce,
sprouted so many spiderweb veins
my legs look like roadmaps.
Despite mother's promises,
this baby has kept her baby fat.

I've taken back every ounce
of every pound I ever lost
and then some. Gravity
has taken over and
thick sweatshirts are a
staple of my wardrobe.

Barbie has been spared the
corrosive effects of aging.
There is no mid-life or senior
incarnation of her, nor
is there a Rasta Barbie or
Goth Barbie. There is only
Flawless Beauty Barbie.

Epilogue: My friend's Barbie died
an unglamorous, bloodless death.
The family's Springer Spaniel
carried her off, buried and
dug her up again and again.
A few passes of a riding mower
finally finished her off.

Rest in pieces, Barbie Doll.

DANCING FOR MISS PATTI

Mom failed her road test twice
and never got her driver's license.
So, I never went anywhere
unless someone else was going, too.
Which is how I ended up taking ballet.

Before ballet, I was a happy
tree-climbing, pollywog poaching,
brawling little tomboy.
But my best friend's mom had a car
and *Wouldn't it be fun if
you girls took ballet together?*
It did not occur to my poor,
deluded mother that, by age ten,
I already outweighed most
ballerinas by twenty pounds.

I had seen Sleeping Beauty
one night on our old Philco.
Ballerinas floated onstage
like dragonflies skimming a lake.
I watched in awe as Fonteyn
in her meringue-like tutu
soared high above the boards
landing in the arms
of a *danseur noble*.
Super Woman wore pointe shoes,
and could hold an arabesque
on a block of cardboard
the size of an ice cube.

I pictured our teacher
as a wispy "bun-head"
with a Russian accent,
who had left behind
a brilliant career just
to bring ballet to us bumpkins.
But Miss Patti was a fleshy,
gum-snapping little blonde
who wore her hair in a poodle cut.
Once a week, she herded us
through our paces
in a dimly lit basement
lined with unforgiving mirrors.

In this hostile space
we routinely brought shame
to the art of Terpsichore.
The steps had fancy French names:
bourré, balancé, plié,
glissade, sissonne, and so on.
I had the physique of a fire plug
and could barely reach the barre.
Turn-out was torture. I landed
my *grand jeté* with a thud
worthy of a Clydesdale.

For reasons yet unknown to me,
we were rewarded after every lesson
with a frothy ice cream soda
at Whelan's Drug Store.
Three years of weekly lessons
followed by infusions of fat grams
only added to my avoirdupois.

My brief sojourn in ballet
taught me only two things:
I would never be a dancer—
and an ice cream soda
was no match for
a strawberry Pavlova.

PAS DE CHAT

She slips and sluices
through my legs,
her long tail carried high.
It shudders like a signal flag
in a stiff sea breeze.
Sabrina Sherpa,
feline *extraordinaire*,
vaults to my desk
eclipsing the monitor
with her gun-metal silhouette.
Mistress, I require
your immediate
and undivided attention,
she whispers through
her sonorous purr.
Arching and stretching
into a graceful arabesque,
she treads my keyboard
and sullies my document
with cat gibberish.
Dominatrix that she is,
she batters my face
with her elegant little head,
then clambers to my shoulders
and coils 'round my neck
like a pesky serpent.
Purring in two-part harmony,
half whisper, half whistle,
she kneads my bare flesh,
unmindful in her ecstasy,
of my exquisite pain.
When I move, she leaps
back to the desk,
snaking and shimmying,
collapsing and rolling.
Papers, pens and books
rain to the floor.
I gently seize her lithe body
grown strangely leaden.
She crouches, Sphinx-like,
her golden orbs narrowing
in baleful reproach.

MYSTERY IN AISLE 23

My Kroger is not where foodies
shop for sumac and saffron.
No strange ingredients on the shelves,
just strange, colorful people.
Guatemalan Indians carrying
babies in slings. Tall Senegalese
women in colorful cottons
and towering headdresses
chatting away in Wolof.
There are dare-devil teenage boys
racing Bascarts up and down
the aisles, mounting and riding
them twenty feet or more.
Their antics feel menacing to me,
and I find myself secretly wishing
one of them would fall on his ass.

I pull a bag of frozen okra
from the freezer case but,
before I can move on, a large
woman, without a word,
plants herself in front of me
and refuses to budge.
Her eyes are shielded by large,
mirror lens sunglasses. On her head,
a garish wig, streaked neon purple,
gold and green—Mardi Gras colors.
Except it's not Mardi Gras.
Before I can say a word,
she speaks: *Say, hon, you got
seven dollars you can lend me?*

I am stunned, never having been
panhandled in a super market.
Her cart is loaded with much more
than seven dollars can buy.

I let her down easy. She shrugs
and wishes me a blessed day.
That's alright, baby.

I have not seen her since.
I only wish I had asked,
why seven dollars?

SUNDAY RUNDOWN

At the foot of the driveway,
I peel the blue plastic skin
from the Sunday Times
and take inventory. A missing
Magazine or Book Review will
provoke a day-long pout.

To stoke my masochistic streak,
I attempt the cockamamie crossword.
In ink. Careful not to bear down.
I must exercise my brain
or risk eventual confinement
to the memory care wing
of some shabby nursing home.

Hungry cats disrupt my struggle.
I pause to feed them the very best.
But they only care if I don't feed
them at all. I imagine a wildcat
strike, my cats picketing,
waving cardboard signs:
"Will feign affection for food."

In the Book Review: a book on
the scorched earth approach
to organizing one's space.
The author exhorts us to
throw out everything
that does not "spark joy."

I survey my cluttered landscape
and wonder what would remain.

GOOD CANDY

They showed up at school one day,
a red-headed brother and sister.
People called them hillbillies,
and that sounded like a bad thing.
They talked kind of funny,
but they were friendly and smiled a lot.
Daddy warshed deeshes at the gin mill.
Mommy scrubbed floors and tended
the hotel rooms above the bar.
Leftovers from the restaurant
kept food on their table.
The rest of us kids couldn't
figure out how they could be so happy
with so little: no TV, no comic books,
no trips to the Dairy Queen,
the movies or the Five and Dime.

When Halloween rolled around,
we trolled the neighborhood
looking to score the good candy:
Milky Ways, Sugar Babies,
Tootsie Pops and M&Ms.
We had to know they were too poor
to give out treats, but that didn't stop us.
We invaded their tiny bungalow
like an army of ravenous mice,
our goodie bags gaping wide.

Daddy was ready for us
He took his shiny old fiddle
down from the wall and,
cradling it like a newborn,
worked the bow over the strings
with his long, red fingers.
We wondered at this strange music
that filled our senses and set his
rail-thin body to rocking,
his foot to tapping. By the time
he finished playing, we were full.

Then, one day they left, as quietly
as they had come. Why they left or where
they ended up, no one seemed to know.
After many years, that nameless mountain air
still sweetens my memory—
more than any good candy.

CONFESSIONS OF A PART-TIME MOURNER

On a daily basis, I am compelled
to read Journey's End,
my newspaper's linguistic fig leaf
for the death notices column.

I focus my morbid curiosity
on the younger ones first.
But some photos are decades old,
and I feel strangely hoodwinked
when I learn the fair young woman
in the grainy photo
made it through 88 winters.

You grew up on a northern Ohio farm
and must have been in your teens
when you married the late Gershon.
Together, you raised dairy cows
and your six surviving children.
You spent your last five years
in a nursing home.
I want to believe your children
didn't let you languish,
that they visited often
and still revered the woman
who gave them light.

I want to think you were alive
and feisty to the end,
even had fits of temper
and lobbed your jelly-breads
at perky candy-stripers

When you left this world,
did you go out with a whimper,
or did you look Death in the maw,
screaming and spitting,
and fight for more time?

However it ended,
you had years enough
to see your hair turn grey
and watch the wrinkles etch
your downy cheeks.

Other lives on this page
shut down far too soon.
They perished in car crashes,
drowned in rivers while fishing,
or stopped a stray bullet
on a mean city street.
Fate flipped the OFF switch,
letting them die with their gifts unspent.

I exhale slowly…
and thank God for missing me again.

BREAKFAST AT HALF DAY CAFÉ

We meet at the café known
for its sweet potato pancakes
and stuffed French toast.
He places his lumbar roll
on the banquette and sits gingerly.
I tell him about my bursitis.
He trumps me with ruptured disks.
We splash pancakes with maple syrup,
bemoan our personal decay.
Trim, tight suburbanites
jog past our window-side table,
trailing trendy pure-bred dogs.
He despairs of his spare tire
and loss of mobility.
I counter with a diatribe
on diet disasters.

We attack our breakfasts with gusto.
Folks in the next Zip Code can hear
our arteries slamming shut.
We digress from memory loss,
depression and decrepitude
to visit the subject of his children,
all doing well: young, vital
and very healthy, thank you.

Soon, the conversation returns
to cholesterol, lipid levels,
charlatan chiropractors,
physical therapy, hydrotherapy
and psychotherapy.

Each medical sub-specialty
warrants another cup of coffee—
we have lost count.
The silly waitress asks,
Will there be anything else?

Tiny beads of syrup dot his shirt.
My bosom is dusted with powdered sugar.
I have eaten enough breakfast
to power a stevedore through his day—
and put artificial sweetener
in my four cups of coffee.

We lumber to the cash register to pay our tabs and agree to do this again.

Soon.

POLAR VORTEX

Our TV weather prophet,
cheerful and warm
against the sinister backdrop
of his satellite weather map,
issues a blizzard
of dire warnings: frostbite,
frozen pipes, cracked
windshields and black ice.
We are to cover all
exposed skin and layer up
in fleece and down until
we can barely move.

The scimitar moon
fades to black.
Lint balls of snow swirl,
followed by sleet,
then freezing rain.
A glassy veneer forms
on roads, sidewalks,
gutters and eaves.
My old dog bolts out the door
and belly-flop slides
down the icy steps.
The crusted snow
caves under his footfall
as he runs laps around the yard.
He staggers back up the steps
and shakes himself off,
strafing me with bits of ice.

The TV drones on as we settle
on the sofa and fall asleep.
I dream of molting my layers
in the warm summer sun.
He dreams of younger legs
and slower squirrels.

Joanne Greenway was born and raised in rural upstate New York and initially embarked on an academic career. She received her MA in French Literature in 1971 from IU Bloomington. In 1973, she began a social service career at the Hamilton County Welfare Department (as it was then called). Thirty years later came retirement and, soon afterward, widowhood. It was that loss which led her to a women's writing group focused on writing as a way to process one's grief. She has been published online and in *For a Better World* (an anthology of poems and drawings centered on the theme of social justice) and has taken honorable mentions in several poetry competitions. *Limited Engagement* is her first published chapbook.

Much of her poetry draws on recent and recovered memories of small town life and growing up in a colorful Italian-American family. Among her many interests: enjoying the creative and performing arts, the study of foreign languages, cats and, of course, books.

www.ingramcontent.com/pod-product-compliance
Lightning Source LLC
Chambersburg PA
CBHW060223050426
42446CB00013B/3150